Journey to the Center of the Earth
Lit Link

Grades 7-8

Written by Krista McMillen
Illustrated by Ric Ward and S&S Learning Materials

About the author: Krista McMillen is a teacher living in Estevan, Saskatchewan with her husband and two young children. She has taught grades 3, 4 and 5/6 as well as Special Education.

ISBN 978-1-55035-863-6
Copyright 2007
All Rights Reserved * Printed in Canada

Published in the United States by:
On The Mark Press
3909 Witmer Road PMB 175
Niagara Falls, New York
14305
www.onthemarkpress.com

Published in Canada by:
S&S Learning Materials
15 Dairy Avenue
Napanee, Ontario
K7R 1M4
www.sslearning.com

At a Glance

Learning Expectations	Chapters 1–4	Chapters 5–8	Chapters 9–12	Chapters 13–16	Chapters 17–20	Chapters 21–24	Chapters 25–28	Chapters 29–32	Chapters 33–36	Chapters 37–39	Chapters 40–43	Chapters 44–46
Reading Comprehension												
• Identify and describe story elements	●											●
• Summarize events and details		●	●	●		●	●	●	●		●	
Reasoning & Critical Thinking Skills												
• Use a Venn diagram to compare/contrast								●				●
• Compare and understand characters		●					●	●		●		
• Use context clues			●				●		●			
• Make inferences	●	●		●	●		●		●	●		
• Understand and identify colloquialisms		●										
• Develop opinions and interpretations		●		●	●	●			●		●	●
• Write a short story									●			
• Write and perform a skit												●
• Create a scale drawing					●							
• Use and label a map			●					●	●	●	●	●
• Create a cryptogram	●											
• Create visual art			●							●		●
• Identify conflict												●
• Create a timeline		●										●
• Conduct and present research		●			●	●	●	●				
• Identify climax												●
• Identify foreshadowing	●											
Language Skills												
• Identify synonyms, homonyms									●	●		
• Identify parts of speech					●	●						●
• Identify syllables			●									
• Identify similes				●								
• Use descriptive words and phrases	●								●			
• Use dictionary or thesaurus skills	●	●	●	●	●	●	●	●	●	●	●	●
• Identify plurals				●								
• Use correct punctuation and capitalization									●			

Journey to the Center of the Earth

Table of Contents

Journey to the Center of the Earth

Overall Learning Expectations

The student will:

- develop and practice their skills in reading, writing, listening and oral communication

- use good literature as a vehicle for developing skills required by curriculum expectations: reasoning, critical, and creative thinking, knowledge of language structure, vocabulary building, and use of conventions

- develop a love for literature and reading

- identify elements of story

- develop personal opinions and interpretations

- develop their ability to express themselves orally to present opinions and information

- develop their ability to work cooperatively with others

- practice good organization skills

- learn about overcoming personal obstacles, personal relationships, character and integrity, and other personality traits

- appreciate that growth in one's character is important

- relate their reading to their own lives and experiences

Journey to the Center of the Earth

List of Skills

Vocabulary Development

1. Use context clues
2. Understand and identify colloquialisms
3. Identify synonyms, antonyms, homonyms
4. Identify adjectives and adverbs
5. Identify syllables
6. Identify similes
7. Use descriptive words and phrases
8. Dictionary or thesaurus skills
9. Identify plurals
10. Use correct punctuation and capitalization

Plot Activities

1. Identify and describe literary elements
2. Summarize events and details
3. Identify climax
4. Identify foreshadowing
5. Identify conflict

Character Activities

1. Compare and understand characters
2. Match characters to their quotes

Creative and Critical Thinking

1. Use a Venn diagram to compare/contrast
2. Make inferences
3. Develop opinions and interpretations
4. Create a cryptogram
5. Create a timeline
6. Conduct and present research

Art Activities

1. Write a short story
2. Write and perform a skit
3. Create visuals of the reading

Integrating Other Subject Areas

1. Create a scale drawing
2. Use and label a map
3. Conduct and present research

Teacher Suggestions

Reading and understanding is a complicated act and requires a variety of different skills. The experience is different for each student. Completing a novel and activities such as those provided in this resource requires student motivation and interest. The activities are designed to be interesting and motivating to students and attempt to apply the novel to their daily lives. Teacher interest and excitement for the novel increases student motivation and interest as well. Each teacher and each class is unique. Use this resource in your own way as a vehicle to create in your students a love for literature, learning and sharing responses with others.

Note: This resource is based on the Bantom Dell, 1991 edition, reissued in May 2006, with an Introduction by Kim Stanley Robinson

Journey to the Center of the Earth

This resource can be used in a variety of ways:

1. The student booklet focuses on several chapters of the novel at one time. These sections contain the following activities:

   a) **Before you Read:** critical thinking, making predictions, and personal development
   b) **Vocabulary Activities:** dictionary and thesaurus use to build vocabulary and language
   c) **Questions on the Chapters:** reading comprehension and interpretation
   d) **Language Activities:** grammar, word structure, sentence structure, literacy skills
   e) **Extension Activities:** creative and critical thinking, research, integration to other subject areas

2. The teacher may read the novel with the class or students may read the novel individually or in "book clubs".

3. **Bulletin Board and Interest Center Ideas:** Earth science (rocks, layers of the Earth, etc.), the animal kingdom, volcanoes, biology, scientists, maps, languages

4. **The Student Checklist:** can be used either by the teacher to record grades or by the student to record completed assignments, or by both

5. Students should not be expected to complete all the assignments. Teachers should **allow some choices** and match the activity to the student's ability.

6. **Integration into other subject areas:** it would be a good idea to plan science and social studies units that fit with the novel at the same time. Some examples of possible units include rocks, earth science, animals and organisms, volcanoes, plants, cultures around the world, electricity, inventions, or personal development and overcoming obstacles.

7. **Collaborative or Cooperative Learning:** this approach is beneficial to student learning. Some ideas for using this approach include book clubs (reading together and splitting up the workload for that chapter), partner work on questions, and completing the visual activities, skits, extension activities and research activities in pairs or small groups.

8. **Independent Reading or Differentiated Learning:** Certain students or all students may be allowed to work at their own pace, handing in activities as they finish.

9. **Fine Arts Activities:** Students can integrate such topics as cultural cooking and social conventions. Favorite sections can be made into skits and video performances or visual art for display.

Journey to the Center of the Earth

10. Students should keep all their work together in one portfolio, binder or duotang to practice **good organization** skills. They will need a notebook or loose leaf paper or other materials for some of the activities as well as the student reproducible booklet.

11. Some students may require some **adaptations** to the material provided such as using a scribe to write the answers as student dictates, having someone read the novel and assignments to or with the student, listening to the book on tape or CD, reducing the quantity to be completed, changing assignments as necessary to fit the student, changing due dates to allow for extra time for students who may work more slowly, communication with the home about a homework program, working in partners, changing the presentation of assignments so that the student can use their strongest learning style to show their understanding or any other adaptation the teacher feels is appropriate to enable the student's success and enjoyment of this wonderful story.

12. In the section for Chapters 9-12 it is recommended that students begin keeping a **Danish – English Dictionary**. If you choose to have students do this as they read, you may want them to create an alphabetized dictionary or simply write the words in the order they read them into the page provided in this booklet.

13. **Assessment:** the student checklist is provided as one way of recording student progress and assessing student work. The teacher may choose which activities to assess and exactly how to complete the assessment for those activities.

14. **At A Glance, Overall Expectations, List of Skills:** These are provided as a reference for the skills and objectives taught through this resource. It is important to cross-reference these with your own curriculum.

15. The **Vocabulary Activities** can be done before reading so students are familiar with the vocabulary in the chapters before they read them, and may as a result, get more out of the reading. It can also be beneficial to read through the questions before reading the chapters so students can be looking for the answers as they read. This is a good organization technique for some students but can be a distraction from the real reading experience for others.

Journey to the Center of the Earth

Synopsis

Journey to the Center of the Earth is the story of Axel Lidenbrock, nephew of the distinguished German scientist, Professor Otto Lidenbrock. It begins on Sunday May 24, 1863, in the Lidenbrock house in Hamburg, Germany. Professor Lidenbrock has just purchased an original runic manuscript. While looking through the book, Lidenbrock and Axel find a coded note written in runic script. Lidenbrock and Axel translate the runic characters into Latin letters, revealing a message written in code. Axel accidentally reveals the answer to the code, although he wants to hide the meaning from his uncle. It is a medieval note written by the Icelandic Arne Saknussemm, who claims to have discovered a passage to the center of the Earth through a volcano called Snaefell in Iceland.

Professor Lidenbrock is an impatient man, and immediately decides to leave for Iceland, taking Axel with him. Axel is less than enthused about going and repeatedly tries to explain his fears of descending into a volcano and discusses various scientific theories as to why the journey is a bad idea. He is unable to be heard by Professor Lidenbrock. Soon they find themselves in Iceland and hire Hans Bjelke (a Danish-speaking eiderdown hunter) as their guide. They travel to the volcano and eventually are able to enter it and set off on their journey.

During their travels inside the Earth they encounter many strange phenomena and dangers. After taking a wrong turn, the three run out of water and Axel nearly dies. Hans discovers a subterranean river (which they name the "Hansbach") and they are saved. After descending many miles, following the course of the Hansbach, they reach an amazingly vast cavern. This underground world is lit by electrically-charged gas, and filled with a vast ocean. The travelers build a raft and set sail on the ocean. While on the water, they see several prehistoric creatures and are nearly eaten by some of them. A lightning storm also threatens their lives, but instead throws them onto the coastline where they realize they have come back to their point of origin. However, on this beach they discover prehistoric plants and animals including a herd of mastodons. On a beach covered with bones, Axel discovers an oversized human skull. Axel and his uncle walk further into the prehistoric forest, and discover a prehistoric human, more than 12 feet in height.

The travelers continue to explore the beach and find a passageway marked by Saknussemm as the way ahead. However, it is blocked by what appears to be a recent cave-in. The travelers blast the rock, but the explosion is larger than they expect and they are swept away into a large open gap in the ground. After spending hours being swept along at high speeds by the water, the raft ends up inside a large cavern filling with water and magma. They are rushed upwards, through burning heat, and ejected onto the surface of the earth. They discover that they have been thrown out of Stromboli, a volcano at the southern tip of Italy. They return home to great acclaim – Professor Lidenbrock is hailed as one of the great scientists of history, Axel marries his sweetheart Graüben, and Hans eventually returns to his peaceful life in Iceland. At the end of the book, Axel and Lidenbrock realize that their compass was behaving strangely after their journey on the raft because they had been struck by lightning, and that they had indeed passed through the very center of the Earth.

Journey to the Center of the Earth

Author Biography

Jules Gabriel Verne was born on February 8, 1828 in Nantes, France. He was the oldest of five children. His father was a lawyer who was precise about everything and known for his honesty. His mother, Sophie Allotte, came from a family of ship builders and sea captains. Jules was close to his brother, Paul. They liked to read travel magazines and imagine journeys. Jules's father wanted him to be a lawyer, but Jules wanted to be a writer. In 1848 he went to Paris with a friend to attempt to sell his work. He had little success at first but continued to write anyway. He met the famous authors Victor Hugo and Alexander Dumas who inspired him. Jules tried to write about history but did not enjoy it. He had very little money so he started going to the public library because it was free and he could keep warm. He spent all day reading about natural science and technology and taking hundreds of notes.

When he went to a friend's wedding, he met Honorine Morel who was a widow with two daughters. They got married and he took a job as a stockbroker. His wife supported his writing but he continued to have little success. In 1881 his only child, Michel was born. In 1863 a blimp-like machine was invented. Jules thought it would be better to invent a balloon that could go up and down with the wind. He used all his knowledge about balloon flight to write a story called *Five Weeks in a Balloon*. It was refused by publishers because it was too scientific and not exciting or adventurous enough. Jules wanted to destroy it but Honorine saved it. In time, Jules rewrote and improved the story. The plot moved faster and was full of adventure. This book was so popular that it was translated into other languages and Jules Verne became rich.

Jules Verne continued to write many important books, basing his novels on the latest scientific knowledge. In 1864 he wrote *Journey to the Center of the Earth*. Then he took some time off to enjoy his wealth but soon got bored. His next book, *From the Earth to the Moon* was about the first space capsule. In 1869 he wrote *20,000 Leagues Under the Sea* about a submarine which was propelled by electricity. (The electric light bulb came eleven years after the book.) In 1870 Jules read a claim that you could go around the world in 90 days and got the idea for his most popular book ever, *Around the World in Eighty Days*. Toward the end of his life Jules realized modern technology could be dangerous. In 1889 he wrote with his son, Michel, *The Diary of an American Journalist* in the Year 2890. It is a story about New York in the future when the press is powerful, depicting huge skyscrapers, rolling sidewalks, TV-telephones, air cars, air trains and electric calculating machines.

Jules Verne was an amazing writer who predicted the science future of the world. Some of the inventions he imagined were created later in his lifetime and some are yet to be invented. He was popular with a variety of readers: rich, poor, young, old, scientists, artists and rulers. He wrote over 80 books mostly before 1900 and a few of the things he described were: helicopters, modern weapons, movies with sound, television and rockets.

Jules Verne died on March 24, 1905 and the whole world mourned. He was the founder of modern science fiction and the creator of many imaginary inventions that became reality. His work continues to inspire scientists, explorers, engineers and writers around the world.

Journey to the Center of the Earth

Student checklist

Name: _____

Assignment	Grade/Level	Comments

Journey to the Center of the Earth

Name: _____

Journey to the Center of the Earth

Chapters 1 to 4

Before you read the chapters:

1. This novel was originally written in French. How do you think the meaning of the text might be affected when translated to English?

   _____

   _____

   _____

2. What do you already know about the Earth?

   _____

   _____

   _____

   _____

Vocabulary:

Use a dictionary to learn the meanings of the following words from these chapters and then write a sentence using the word. Make sure the meaning of the word is understood from the sentence.

1. culinary: _____

   _____

2. irascible: _____

   _____

3. obstinate: _____

   _____

4. incessantly: _____

   _____

5. calumny: _____

   _____

6. façade: _____

   _____

 # Journey to the Center of the Earth

7. curator: _____
_____

8. savant: _____
_____

9. irrefragable: _____
_____

10. beguiled: _____
_____

Questions:

1. Where is this story set? _____
_____

2. Describe Otto Lidenbrock using adjectives and descriptions from the book as well as your own. Tell his occupation and describe how he was treated by the townspeople.
_____
_____
_____

3. Describe the house where Professor Lidenbrock lived. Tell who lived in the house with him.
_____
_____
_____

4. Axel is the main character in our story. We learn a lot about him by what he says and his actions. What are some of the things we know about him by the end of Chapter 4?
_____
_____

5. Describe the book Professor Lidenbrock found.
_____
_____
_____

Journey to the Center of the Earth

6. At first Axel is not very interested by Professor Lidenbrock's book; in fact he is faking his enthusiasm to please his uncle. By Chapter 4 Axel has caught some of the Professor's enthusiasm and passion to find the solution. What do we know about the Professor and Axel and their relationship from their behavior?

_____

_____

_____

7. What was Axel's relationship with Grauben?

_____

_____

8. What is Axel doing when he suddenly realizes the solution to the cryptogram? What is his reaction when he reads the deciphered code and what does he plan to do with the document?

_____

_____

_____

_____

Language Activity:

Literary Elements

Tone: The *attitude* conveyed by the writing, for example, ironic, cynical, sarcastic, humorous, mysterious, creepy, straight-forward, matter-of-fact, exciting, boring, serious, fun, informative, instructional, etc.

Mood: The way the story makes you *feel*, for example, happy, sad, worried, scared, excited, angry, anxious, etc.

Point of View: The voice telling the story. There are three possible points of view; **first person** is narrated by one character in the story so we can only know that person's feelings and thoughts; **third person** is narrated by an outsider who tells what is happening but cannot tell us feelings or thoughts of the characters; or **omniscient** is an all-knowing voice that can tell us what is happening, what all characters are thinking, feeling and doing.

Foreshadowing: The author subtly suggests or hints about future events to happen in the story.

Journey to the Center of the Earth

After reading about these literary elements answer the questions below:

1. What do you think is the tone of this novel so far? _____
2. What do you think is the mood of this novel so far? _____
3. What do you think the point of view is? _____
4. There are two examples of foreshadowing in this section (pages 9 and 16). Find them and write the sentence from the book that foreshadows possible future events of the book.

   Page 9: _____
   _____

   Page 16: _____
   _____

Extension Activity:

Write your own Cryptogram!

In the novel a cryptogram is described as:

"A message where the "sense is concealed by a deliberate jumbling of the letters, which would make an intelligible sentence if they were correctly rearranged."

Now create your own cryptogram. Decide on a decoding method. Some examples are: having numbers stand for letters, reversing the alphabet, creating different symbols to stand for letters, etc. Your cryptogram must be one sentence long – at least 5 words. When you are done, share your cryptogram with a classmate to see if he or she can decipher it!

Your decoding method:

   a b c d e f g h i j k l m n o p q r s t u v w x y z
   _____

Your sentence in English:
   _____
   _____

Your cryptogram:
   _____
   _____

Journey to the Center of the Earth

Chapters 5 to 8

Before you read the chapters:

1. How long do you think you could hold out without any water or food while trying to keep a secret? _____

2. Have you ever had a fear of heights or any other fears? Do you think you could face your fear and overcome it if someone forced you to? _____
_____

Vocabulary:

Match the number of each word to the correct definition.

1.	indefatigable	____ very hungry
2.	inadvertence	____ a burden
3.	voracious	____ someone taking part in a conversation
4.	imprecations	____ to sway back and forth
5.	interlocutor	____ weak, clumsy, disabled
6.	kalends/calends	____ incorrect/wrong
7.	erroneous	____ turned upside down
8.	portmanteau	____ a supportive railing
9.	descried	____ dizziness
10.	dissuade	____ a steep mass of rock
11.	encumbrance	____ evil curses placed upon someone
12.	sundry	____ a fortress to protect citizens
13.	anathematize	____ to advise against
14.	berth	____ cannot make tired
15.	polygot	____ the first day of a new month
16.	precipice	____ to proclaim a curse upon
17.	quays	____ a room on a ship
18.	citadel	____ one who can speak many languages
19.	traversed	____ all different kinds, various
20.	balustrade	____ walked through or along
21.	oscillate	____ to have noticed, to have seen
22.	abyss	____ a deep hole that goes on and on
23.	vertigo	____ wharfs where ships are loaded
24.	inversion	____ a suitcase
25.	lame	____ not done intentionally

Journey to the Center of the Earth

Questions:

1. At the end of Chapter 4 Axel discovered the solution to the cryptogram. Why did he choose not to tell his uncle?

   _____

   _____

2. How long did Axel hold out before he finally revealed the answer to his uncle? What finally caused him to do so?

   _____

   _____

3. a) Why did Axel object to the journey? How did he feel about going?

   _____

   _____

   _____

   b) How do you think you would feel if you were asked to go on a journey such as this one?

   _____

   _____

4. In Chapter 6 Axel tells his uncle that he believes the document may be just a hoax. What are Axel's reasons for thinking so? (pages 25 - 28)

   _____

   _____

   _____

   _____

5. On page 32 Grauben tells Axel, "....I would gladly accompany you and your uncle, but a poor girl like me would only be an encumbrance." (Remember that this was written over 100 years ago when views about women were very different.) Below, write a response you think Grauben would say today.

   _____

   _____

6. When Axel was leaving, Grauben encouraged him to go even though it was difficult for her to see him go. What were her parting words to him?

   _____

   _____

Journey to the Center of the Earth

7. Write a timeline of Axel and Professor Lidenbrock's travels from Altona, Germany to Copenhagen, Denmark.

   _____

   _____

8. What did Axel think about as he toured around the town of Copenhagen?

   _____

9. **a)** Why did the professor want to climb the steeple of the church, Vor-Frelsers Kirk?

   _____

   _____

   b) What was this experience like for Axel?

   _____

   c) How many days did they do this?

   _____

10. Professor Lidenbrock is successful in his search for a vessel to take them to Iceland. What is the name of this vessel and the captain? When are they scheduled to be on board?

    _____

    _____

Language Activities:

Colloquialisms:

A **colloquialism** is a word or phrase that is not usually used in formal speech or writing. It is similar to slang. It can be one word or a phrase or saying which might compare one thing to another. Colloquialisms are often associated with a certain place or area of the world. A person must have some common understanding in order to understand the colloquialism. For example on page 23 Axel describes his uncle, ".. as if suddenly touched by a Leyden jar." If you do not know what a Leyden jar is, you will not be able to understand this colloquial saying.

1. Do some research in your library or on the Internet to find out what a Leyden jar is.

   _____

   _____

Journey to the Center of the Earth

2. Now try to think of some of the colloquialisms you know. Write as many as you can think of below.

_____
_____
_____
_____
_____

Extension Activities:

1. On page 19 Axel describes how many combinations 20 letters could form. Try to write the number he describes in standard form below.

_____

2. Arne Saknussemm was Icelandic. Icelandic is a very old Norse culture and language. Do some research in your library or on the Internet to find out more about the Icelandic language and culture. Some of your research might include: How are children named in this culture? Do women change their names when they marry? What are some of the cities in Iceland? What is unique about the days and nights in Iceland? What were the first settlers in Iceland like? What are the letters of their alphabet and some words in Icelandic? Your teacher may want you to present your findings to the class.

_____
_____
_____
_____
_____
_____
_____
_____
_____
_____
_____
_____
_____
_____
_____
_____
_____
_____
_____

Journey to the Center of the Earth

Chapters 9 to 12

Before you read the chapters:

1. Axel and the professor are about to go on a very exciting journey. How do you feel before going on a big trip?

   _____

2. What do you think might happen in the next few chapters?

   _____

   _____

Vocabulary:

You can often figure out the meaning of a word from the context of the sentence in which it is written. Read the sentences below and look them up in your book. Write what you think the bold word means from the sentence. Then write the dictionary definition. How close were your definitions to the actual meaning?

1. page 43 – "It is now used as a **sumptuous** lodge for the toll-keeper for the Sound..."

   Your definition: _____

   Dictionary: _____

   _____

2. page 44 – "She was loaded with coal for Reikiavik, and household utensils, **earthenware**, woolen clothing, and a cargo of wheat."

   Your definition: _____

   Dictionary: _____

   _____

3. page 47 – "A church rose between the little lake and the town, built in the Protestant style and with **calcined** stones which the volcanoes brought up from the earth at their own expense."

   Your definition: _____

   Dictionary: _____

   _____

Journey to the Center of the Earth

4. page 47 – "On a neighboring **eminence** I perceived the national school where, as I was subsequently informed by our host, Hebrew, English, French and Danish are taught; four languages of which, I am ashamed to say, I didn't know a single word."

   Your definition: _____

   Dictionary: _____

   _____

5. page 52 – "All he managed, however, was a sort of **diabolical** grin."

   Your definition: _____

   Dictionary: _____

   _____

6. page 55 – "This grave, **phlegmatic**, silent personage was named Hans Bjilke."

   Your definition: _____

   Dictionary: _____

   _____

7. page 57 – "A **chronometer** by Boisonas, jun., of Geneva, accurately regulated by the meridian of Hamburg."

   Your definition: _____

   Dictionary: _____

   _____

8. page 57 – "Then there were **provisions**. But these did not take up much room, though it was comforting to know we had enough essence of beef and dry biscuits to last us six months."

   Your definition: _____

   Dictionary: _____

   _____

9. page 60 – "Often these chains of barren rocks made a sharp turn towards the sea, **encroaching** on the pasturage, but there was always room enough to pass."

    Your definition:_____

    Dictionary:_____

    _____

10. page 63 – "However intelligent our horses might be, I did not **augur** anything good from attempting to cross a regular arm of the sea on the back of a quadruped."

    Your definition:_____

    Dictionary:_____

    _____

Questions:

1. M. Thomson gave letters of introduction to give to the governor, the suffragan, and the mayor of Iceland. Why was this helpful?

    _____

    _____

2. **a)** What was the trip from Denmark to Iceland like for the Professor?

    _____

    b) What did Axel mean when he said, "It must be owned he rather deserved his fate."?

    _____

3. From the description of Reikiavik on page 47 do you think Reikiavik is a place you would like to visit? Why or why not?

    _____

    _____

4. **a)** Describe how the people of Reikiavik use library books.

    _____

    b) What does M. Fridrickson say about how Icelanders feel about reading and learning?

    _____

Journey to the Center of the Earth

5. What happened to Arne Saknussemm and his writings?

_____

_____

6. Why was the Professor hiding his knowledge of Snaefell and Arne Saknussemm from M. Fridrikson and the others?

_____

_____

7. Reread the description of Hans on page 54. Now draw a picture of him in the space below from that description.

```



```

8. What instruments, arms, tools, provisions and other items did the travelers take with them?

_____

_____

9. What does Axel mean when he says on page 59, "...I began to take my share in the business."?

_____

_____

10. Does Axel believe he is going to the center of the Earth? How do you know?

_____

Journey to the Center of the Earth

Language Activities:

1. Break the following words into syllables using dashes. **Example:** ac-tiv-i-ty

   a) Reikiavik _____

   b) sumptuous _____

   c) Valkyria _____

   d) suffragan _____

   e) mineralogical _____

   f) diabolical _____

   g) precipitous _____

   h) manometer _____

   i) provisions _____

2. Re-read the descriptive paragraphs from the novel in which Axel describes Reikiavik (page 47, 48). Pay attention to the adjectives used to make us feel like we are actually there. After reading these paragraphs write your own descriptive paragraph about an unusual place. It can be a real place you have been or an imaginary place.

3. Sometimes an author makes a reference in his writing which you need to have some knowledge about in order to understand the entire message. Read the following references from the novel. If you do not understand them already, ask someone or do some research to answer the questions that arise.

   a) page 43: "In my excited nervous state I expected to see the ghost of Hamlet wandering on the legendary terrace. 'Sublime madman!' I said to myself. 'You would approve our proceedings, undoubtedly...."
   Who is Hamlet and what is Axel referring to when he says you would approve of our proceedings?

   _____

   _____

   b) page 46: "It was the soft tongue of Horace that he came to offer his services..."
   Who is Horace and what is meant by "the soft tongue..."?

   _____

   _____

 # Journey to the Center of the Earth

c) page 59: "...and that last line of Virgil which seemed to have been made for uncertain travelers on the road, like us: Et quacumque viam dederit fortuna sequamur."
Who is Virgil and what does the saying mean?

_____

_____

Extension Activities:

1. Begin a map showing where Axel and his uncle travel. Use an atlas or the Internet to label the places Axel and his uncle travel. Be sure to include these cities and bodies of water:

Hamburg/Altona, Germany	Snaefell	Kiel
Cape Reikiana	Copenhagen	Great Belt
Stapi	Zealand	Korsor
Portland Bay/Cape Portland	Holstein	Gardar
Skagen	Reikiavik	

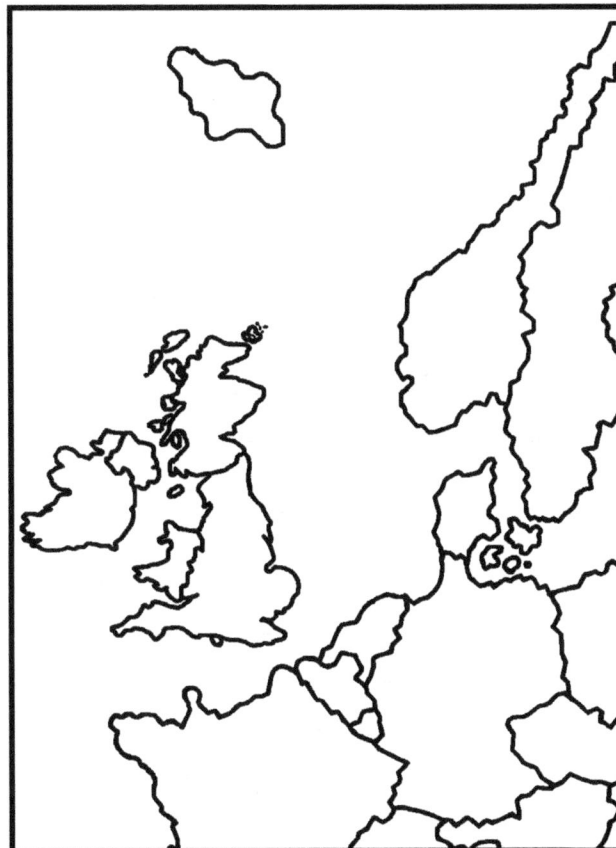

Journey to the Center of the Earth

2. Begin keeping a Danish-English dictionary. Write down the Danish words you learn as you read the novel, along with their English meaning.

Danish-English Dictionary

Journey to the Center of the Earth

Chapters 13 to 16

Before you read the chapters:

1. In Iceland during the summer the sun never sets and it is daylight all day long. How do you think this would affect people who live there and their daily lives?

   _____

   _____

Vocabulary:

Use a thesaurus to find similes for words from these chapters.

Original Word	**Simile**
1. fodder	_____
2. taciturnity	_____
3. spectre	_____
4. gesticulate	_____
5. subterranean	_____
6. herbaceous	_____
7. epoch	_____
8. circuitous	_____
9. truncated	_____
10. protuberance	_____

Many of the vocabulary words in this novel and in these chapters are scientific terms, often earth-science terms. On a separate sheet of paper, make a list of some of the science words in these chapters. Join with a friend to look up the meanings of these words in a dictionary or science text glossary.

Questions:

1. How were the home, the customs and the daily life of the peasant's different from Axel's?

   _____

   _____

Journey to the Center of the Earth

2. Describe the people the travelers came across after they left the peasant's hut.
   _____
   _____

3. What was Axel's final argument to his uncle and what was the professor's response?
   _____
   _____

4. How were the travelers treated by the rector and his wife?
   _____
   _____

5. What was the climb up Snaefell like for Axel? How did the Professor help him?
   _____
   _____

6. How did Hans save the group from the Mistour?
   _____
   _____

7. What did Axel compare to the crater of Snaefell that he was about to enter?
   _____
   _____

8. Why was the professor so upset when he awoke after the first night in the crater to a cloudy sky?
   _____
   _____

9. When and how did they finally get the indication of which direction they were to go?
   _____
   _____

Journey to the Center of the Earth

Language Activities:

Irregular Plural Nouns: Some nouns are pluralized irregularly. Use the irregular plural rules to write the irregular plurals of the science words below.

Singular	Plural	Rule
hypothesis	_____	words ending in es or is: change ending to es
axis	_____	words ending in es or is: change ending to es
bacillus	_____	words ending in us: change us to i
fungus	_____	words ending in us: change us to i
radius	_____	words ending in us: change us to i
phenomenon	_____	words ending in on: change to a
bacterium	_____	words ending in um: change to a
vortex	_____	words ending in ex: change to ices

Extension Activities:

Use the heights of these mountains to create a scale drawing in the chart below to compare some of the world's tallest mountains to Snaefell.

Mt. Everest (Nepal)	29 035 feet (8 850 m)
Mt. McKinley (Alaska/Canada)	20 321 feet (6 194 m)
K2 (Kashmir)	28 251 feet (8 611 m)
Anconcagua (Argentina)	22 841 feet (6 962 m)
Snaefell	5 000 feet (1 524 m)

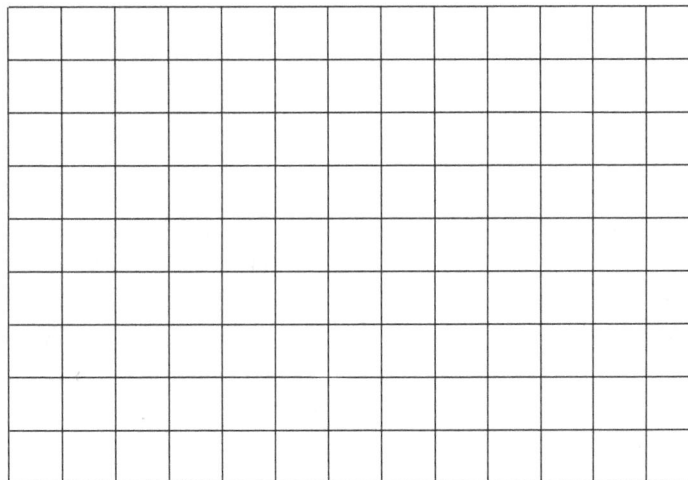

Journey to the Center of the Earth

Chapters 17 to 20

Before you read the chapters:

Imagine you are Axel, about to embark on a journey into the center of the Earth. What are some of the emotions you might be feeling?

_____

_____

Vocabulary Crossword:

The clues below are given along with a page number on which the answer can be found.

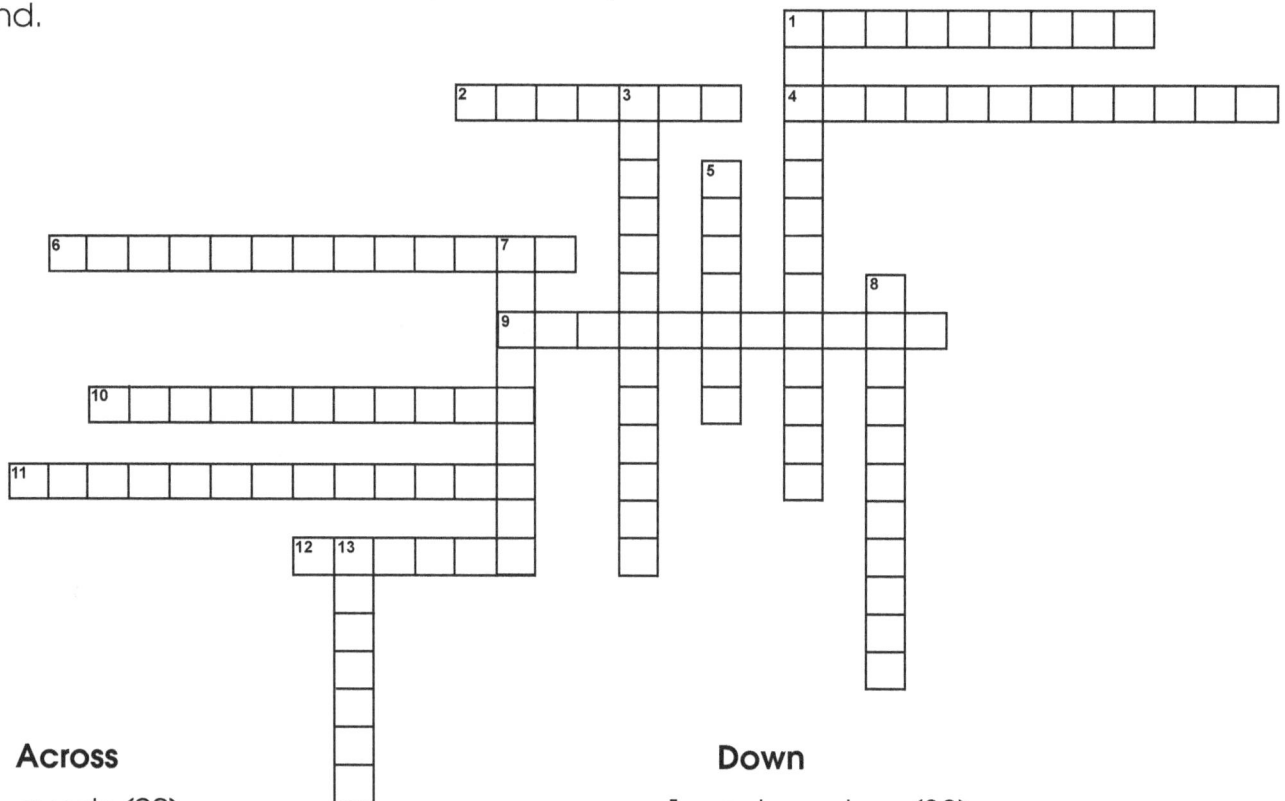

Across

1. guests (90)
2. the order Fucales, algae (96)
4. structural make-up (84)
6. ferns (96)
9. to go directly ahead (91)
10. a state of balance (86)
11. sparkle (88)
12. permeable by water and air (90)

Down

1. noisy outcry (88)
3. not disputable (96)
5. emptiness (84)
7. up against the edge of an object (84)
8. affect control (84)
13. to anticipate and prevent (85)

Journey to the Center of the Earth

Questions:

1. What is the "abyss attraction" Axel talks about in Chapter 17? Have you ever experienced this feeling? If so, tell where.

   _____

   _____

2. Describe the "theory of central heat" and how Professor Lidenbrock planned to disprove it.

   _____

   _____

3. At the end of Chapter 18 the travelers were 10 000 feet below sea level. What was the significance of that distance?

   _____

   _____

4. At the beginning of Chapter 19 the travelers came to a fork in their path. The professor did not hesitate in taking the path to the east. Why did he take this path and what does his reasoning show about his character?

   _____

   _____

5. Axel begins to notice the changes in the rock as they walk through the east tunnel. What do these changes tell Axel about the route they are taking? How does Professor Lidenbrock react to Axel's observations and concerns?

   _____

   _____

   _____

6. How long do the travelers walk along the east path before deciding with absolute certainty that it is the wrong way?

   _____

7. What is the struggle the group must face at the end of Chapter 20?

   _____

Journey to the Center of the Earth

Language Activities:

An adverb is a word that describes a verb. In the activity below you are given a verb and the page number on which you will find it. Once you have found the verb write the adverb that is used to describe it.

Page	Verb	Adverb (How was the action done?)
84	accepted	1. _____
86	clutching	2. _____
87	fell	3. _____
89	descend	4. _____
90	slipping	5. _____
91	ate	6. _____
95	shouldered	7. _____
96	examine	8. _____

Extension Activities:

In these chapters the author introduces many scientific concepts and facts. You may become curious to know more. Do some research to find out more about one of the following topics:

- Facts about the size of the Earth and its interior
- Rock types
- The theory of central heat
- Volcanoes – active and extinct
- Air pressure below the Earth's surface
- Mining – the deepest mines on earth
- The periods of Earth's development – including the Silurian period
- The scientific classification of animals (Kingdom, Phylum, Class, Order, Family, Genus, Species)
- Prehistoric animals

Present your results in a science fair with your class or school.

Journey to the Center of the Earth

Chapters 21 to 24

Before you read the chapters:

In our story the characters must trust and depend on one another to get through the challenges they encounter. Think of a time when you had to depend on someone to get through a difficult challenge. Write about that experience on a separate piece of paper and share it with your class or a friend.

Vocabulary:

Look up the meanings of the following words and then write a sentence showing the meaning of each word.

1. placid: _____

_____

2. stifling: _____

_____

3. inert: _____

_____

4. austere: _____

_____

5. gourd: _____

_____

6. ensued: _____

_____

7. interposed: _____

_____

8. incredulity: _____

_____

9. diminution: _____

_____

Journey to the Center of the Earth

10. myriad: _____

_____

11. inextricable: _____

_____

12. covetous: _____

_____

13. coruscations: _____

_____

14. delectation: _____

_____

15. perilous: _____

_____

16. chasm: _____

_____

Questions:

1. Why did the Professor save some water when it seemed their water supply had run out?

_____

_____

2. What does the Professor propose to do at the end of Chapter 21, and why?

_____

_____

3. Where does Axel initially think Hans is going when he sees him walk away in Chapter 22? What makes him realize his first thought was incorrect?

_____

_____

4. In Chapter 23 the group realizes they are finally near water. How do they know this? How do they tap the source?

_____

_____

Journey to the Center of the Earth

5. a) At the end of Chapter 24, how many leagues have they come from Iceland?

   _____

   b) How far below sea level are they? _____

   c) What part of the world are they below now? _____

6. In what ways did the flowing water remind Axel of both Hans and the Professor?

   _____

Language Activities:

In the activity below, a noun and page number are given. Find the noun on the page given, find the adjective used to describe that noun, and write the adjective below.

Noun	Page	Adjective
lips	102	1. _____
hands	102	2. _____
tears	102	3. _____
voice	103	4. _____
silence	107	5. _____
Icelander	108	6. _____
liquid	109	7. _____
fellow	110	8. _____
guide	113	9. _____
nephew	113	10. _____
road	114	11. _____
granite	115	12. _____

Extension Activities:

At the beginning of this section our travelers are searching for water. If they had not found any water they would not have survived. Do some research to find out why water is so necessary for our bodies. What is it that water provides our bodies? How long can we last without it? Write down the answers to these questions and any other water facts you learn, on a separate sheet of paper.

Journey to the Center of the Earth

Chapters 25 to 28

Before you read the chapters:

Have you ever been lost or separated from someone? Write about your experience and how you felt. How did you eventually find your way and reunite with the person or people you were separated from?

_____

_____

_____

_____

_____

_____

Vocabulary:

Write the letter of the vocabulary word beside its correct meaning.

a) troglodytes   ____ determining a boundary

b) superfluities   ____ harsh

c) sublunary   ____ calmness

d) adroitness   ____ talent in use of hands and body

e) sangfroid   ____ situated on the Earth

f) demarcation   ____ to faint

g) prostrated   ____ usual meaning of a word

h) denizen   ____ a resident

i) swoon   ____ to have thrown oneself face down on the ground in humility

j) succour   ____ animals that live in caves

k) acceptation   ____ luxuries

l) rigorous   ____ assistance, help

Questions:

1. At the beginning of Chapter 25 what part of the inner Earth did Axel and Professor Lidenbrock calculate they had reached? What was the temperature supposed to be and what was the actual temperature?

_____

_____

Journey to the Center of the Earth

2. What would supposedly happen due to decreased pressure once they reached the center of the Earth?

   _____

   _____

3. What did Axel say about being shut up in the tunnel?

   _____

   _____

4. What was Axel's reaction to getting lost?

   _____

   _____

5. What did Axel do to try to find his uncle and Hans again?

   _____

   _____

6. Do you think Axel was reasonable in his reactions to his circumstances? Why or why not?

   _____

   _____

7. How were Axel and his uncle able to hear one another in the "gallery of granite"?

   _____

Journey to the Center of the Earth

Language Activities:

Match the letter of each character to the quotation which was spoken by that character. The quotes are taken from Chapters 1 to 28.

a) Grauben

b) M. Fridrikson

c) Hans

d) Martha

e) Axel

f) Professor Lidenbrock

g) Captain Bjorne

_____ " Goodness me! Then there is nothing for us but starvation?"

_____ "... it is a grand thing to devote oneself to science. What glory awaits Mr. Lidenbrock, and will be reflected in his companion!"

_____ "We are of the opinion that instead of letting books grow moldy behind an iron grating, far from the vulgar gaze, it is better to let them wear out by being read."

_____ "No, M. Lidenbrock. Make your mind easy, we'll get there soon enough."

_____ "Hastigt, hastigt!"

_____ "If we go on at this rate, we should take 2 000 days or nearly five and a half years to descend."

_____ "I am the Columbus of these subterranean regions, and I ask you to give me one more day."

Extension Activities:

Do some research to find out what exactly a league is. In what situations are leagues generally used? What does one league convert to in miles? In kilometers? What you would find 16 leagues below ground?

_____

_____

_____

_____

_____

_____

_____

_____

_____

Journey to the Center of the Earth

Chapters 29 to 32

Before you read the chapters:

Imagine finding a new species of animal. Create a new species of fish or aquatic animal below. Draw a picture of it below and tell about its special characteristics.

_____
_____
_____
_____

Vocabulary:

Write the correct word from the novel to fit the clues below and then find them in the word search.

1. decorated _____
2. healed _____
3. still _____
4. waves _____
5. the wall of a _____
   cliff, cave, ditch, etc.
6. lighted _____
7. the northern lights _____
8. to be certain of _____
9. awareness _____
10. filled with energy _____

11. sloping downward_____
12. small streams _____
13. a high point of land_____
14. a person or animal _____
    who lived before the flood
15. a collection of animals_____
16. like a tree in size and_____
    shape
17. a temporary delusion _____
    or hallucination
18. to examine carefully_____

Journey to the Center of the Earth

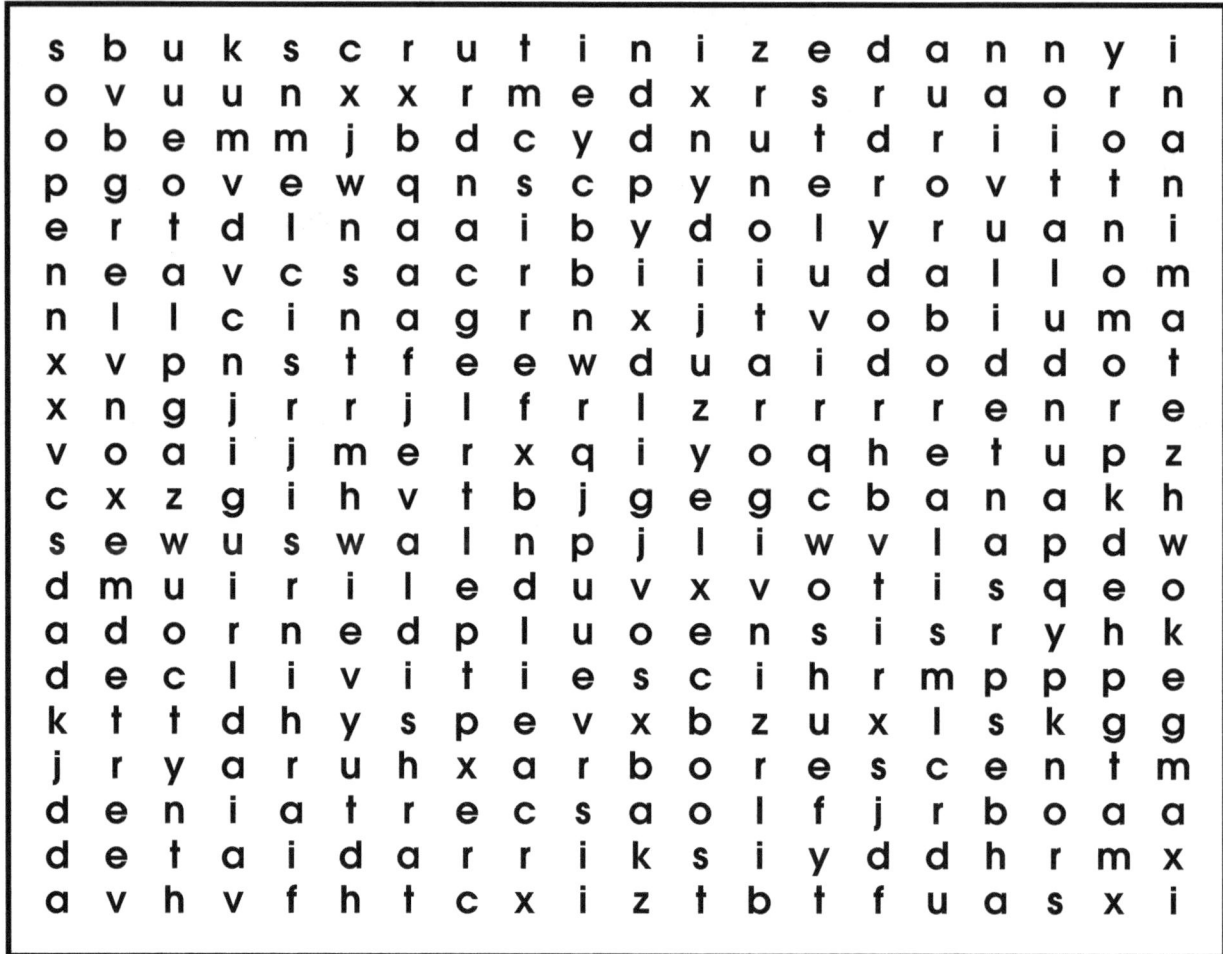

```
s  b  u  k  s  c  r  u  t  i  n  i  z  e  d  a  n  n  y  i
o  v  u  u  n  x  x  r  m  e  d  x  r  s  r  u  a  o  r  n
o  b  e  m  m  j  b  d  c  y  d  n  u  t  d  r  i  i  o  a
p  g  o  v  e  w  q  n  s  c  p  y  n  e  r  o  v  t  t  n
e  r  t  d  l  n  a  a  i  b  y  d  o  l  y  r  u  a  n  i
n  e  a  v  c  s  a  c  r  b  i  i  u  d  a  l  l  o  m
n  l  l  c  i  n  a  g  r  n  x  j  t  v  o  b  i  u  m  a
x  v  p  n  s  t  f  e  e  w  d  u  a  i  d  o  d  d  o  t
x  n  g  j  r  r  j  l  f  r  l  z  r  r  r  e  n  r  e
v  o  a  i  j  m  e  r  x  q  i  y  o  q  h  e  t  u  p  z
c  x  z  g  i  h  v  t  b  j  g  e  g  c  b  a  n  a  k  h
s  e  w  u  s  w  a  l  n  p  j  l  i  w  v  l  a  p  d  w
d  m  u  i  r  i  l  e  d  u  v  x  v  o  t  i  s  q  e  o
a  d  o  r  n  e  d  p  l  u  o  e  n  s  i  s  r  y  h  k
d  e  c  l  i  v  i  t  i  e  s  c  i  h  r  m  p  p  p  e
k  t  t  d  h  y  s  p  e  v  x  b  z  u  x  l  s  k  g  g
j  r  y  a  r  u  h  x  a  r  b  o  r  e  s  c  e  n  t  m
d  e  n  i  a  t  r  e  c  s  a  o  l  f  j  r  b  o  a  a
d  e  t  a  i  d  a  r  r  i  k  s  i  y  d  d  h  r  m  x
a  v  h  v  f  h  t  c  x  i  z  t  b  t  f  u  a  s  x  i
```

Questions:

1. When Axel and Professor Lidenbrock are finally reunited, Axel writes, "but it requires such dangers to excite the professor to such demonstrations." What exactly does he mean by this?

   _____

   _____

2. What did Axel learn about their location when he finally awakened?

   _____

3. What animal remains did they find at first on the beach?

   _____

Journey to the Center of the Earth

4. What did Professor Lidenbrock believe would happen to the compass once they were directly below the North Pole?

    _____

5. What did Hans build the raft of? _____

6. As they were leaving the beach Professor Lidenbrock proposed to give a name to the harbor they left from. What name did he propose and what was Axel's response?

    _____

    _____

7. What are the first living animals they find? _____

Language Activities:

Choose two characters from the novel to compare and contrast. Consider physical appearance, personality, attitude, age, talents, etc. Use the diagram below to show at least three ways they are similar and three ways they are different.

Character 1: _____
Differences: _____

_____

_____

_____

Similarities of both characters:

_____

_____

_____

Character 2: _____
Differences: _____

_____

_____

_____

_____

Journey to the Center of the Earth

Chapters 33 to 36

Before you read the chapters:

Tell what you know about electricity and thunderstorms.

_____
_____
_____

Vocabulary:

Write the letter of the vocabulary word beside its correct meaning.

a) anatomical

b) incandescent

c) approbation

d) concentric

e) cataract

f) acceleration

g) coruscation

h) tranquil

i) preternatural

j) imbibe

k) halyard

l) silicious

m) illumined

n) fluctuating

o) premonitory

p) oppressive

____ a waterfall

____ emitting light

____ drink

____ warning of the future

____ burdensome

____ having a common center

____ rise and fall regularly

____ peaceful, quiet

____ structure of an organism

____ approval

____ an exception to nature

____ speeding up

____ a rope used in sailing

____ rich in silica

____ a flash of light

____ gave light to

Questions:

1. Why was Professor Lidenbrock upset at the beginning of Chapter 33?

_____

Journey to the Center of the Earth

2. Why did they drop the pickaxe into the sea and what did they learn and see when they brought it back up?

   _____

   _____

3. What types of animals did they see as they were afloat on the sea?

   _____

   _____

4. Describe the two reptiles they saw. They were afraid these reptiles would attack them. What happened instead?

   _____

   _____

5. Axel was terrified in Chapter 34. Why was he terrified and what did his source of fear turn out to be?

   _____

   _____

6. Where does Axel believe they are at the end of Chapter 34?

   _____

   _____

7. How does Axel describe the weather before the storm begins?

   _____

   _____

8. Tell about the electrical disc that appears during the storm and how it affects them.

   _____

   _____

9. Tell what the storm was like and how they survive it.

   _____

   _____

   _____

Journey to the Center of the Earth

Language Activities:

Homonyms are words that sound alike but have a different spelling and meaning. Skim the pages of these chapters to find words that are homonyms. Write them below along with their homonym pairs. Find at least eight.

Example: their, there, they're; sea, see

_____   _____   _____   _____
_____   _____   _____   _____
_____   _____   _____   _____
_____   _____   _____   _____

Extension Activities:

Jules Vern created some amazing "never before discovered" animals from his imagination in these chapters. Use your imagination to write a short story about coming face to face with a new and amazing species of animal. Be sure to use a lot of descriptive language so your readers can see the animal in their mind's eye and imagine they are there experiencing the event. You may need more paper.

_____
_____
_____
_____
_____
_____
_____
_____
_____
_____
_____
_____
_____
_____
_____
_____
_____
_____
_____
_____
_____

Journey to the Center of the Earth

Chapters 37 to 39

Before you read the chapters:

In the coming chapters Professor Lidenbrock discovers the greatest scientific finds of his life! What is the "coolest" thing you have ever found? Write about how it felt when you found the item. If you can't think of anything you have actually found, write about something you imagine you would be excited to find.

_____
_____
_____
_____
_____
_____
_____
_____

Vocabulary:

You can often figure out the meaning of a word from the context of the sentence in which it is written. Read the sentences below and look them up in your book. Write what you think the bold word means from the sentence. Then write the dictionary definition. How close were your definitions to the actual meaning?

1. page 163: "The human ear can no longer measure the **increment** of sound."

   Your definition:_____

   Dictionary _____

   _____

2. page 164: "Even a word shouted in the ear was **inaudible**"

   Your definition:_____

   Dictionary:_____

   _____

3. page 165: "…Hans, motionless at the tiller, and 'spitting fire' under the influence of the electricity which **pervaded** his body…"

   Your definition: _____

   Dictionary: _____

   _____

4. page 166: "Even at this time a **deluge** of rain was falling, but with that accumulated force that betokens the end of a storm."

   Your definition: _____

   Dictionary: _____

   _____

5. page 168: "I ought to have been used to my uncle's **eccentricities** by this time, but still they never ceased to surprise me."

   Your definition: _____

   Dictionary: _____

   _____

6. page 169: "…we cannot decide unless we are sure that we have not **deviated** from our course."

   Your definition: _____

   Dictionary: _____

   _____

7. page 170: "Standing upright on the rock, betraying his irritation by his **menacing** attitude, Otto Lidenbrock reminded me of Ajax defying the gods."

   Your definition: _____

   Dictionary: _____

   _____

8. page 171: "But the Icelander seemed to have put away all individual will, and taken a vow of **abnegation**."

Your definition: _____

Dictionary: _____

_____

9. page 175: "These remains, it is true, were not actually human, but **relics** of man's industry…"

Your definition: _____

Dictionary: _____

_____

10. page 176: "…as we gazed at this vast **ossuary** of the 'Sea of Lidenbrock' …"

Your definition: _____

Dictionary: _____

_____

11. page 177: "I had no desire to **contravene** the assertion."

Your definition: _____

Dictionary: _____

_____

12. page 178: "It presents no indication of **prognathism**, which modifies the facial angle."

Your definition: _____

Dictionary: _____

_____

Journey to the Center of the Earth

Questions:

1. What did the travelers lose during the storm? What minor injuries did Axel obtain in the storm.

   _____

   _____

2. How did Professor Lidenbrock plan to get back to the surface of the Earth?

   _____

   _____

3. What did they discover when they looked at the compass in Chapter 37?

   _____

   _____

4. What were Axel's arguments against returning to the raft and the water?

   _____

   _____

5. How does Axel explain the ocean inside the Earth and the electrical activity?

   _____

   _____

6. What did the travelers find at the end of Chapter 38?

   _____

   _____

7. Describe the scientific argument Axel describes at the beginning of Chapter 39 and how it pertains to what they have found.

   _____

   _____

8. How might some of our present technology have made it easier for the Professor to have shown his findings to the world?

   _____

   _____

Journey to the Center of the Earth

Language Activities:

Synonyms are words that have the same or similar meanings. Skim the pages of these chapters to find words that are synonyms. Write them below along with a synonym partner. Find at least eight.

Examples: sound, noise; ceased, stopped

_____ _____ _____ _____
_____ _____ _____ _____
_____ _____ _____ _____
_____ _____ _____ _____

Extension Activities:

The travelers have come across some interesting surroundings below the Earth. Draw a picture of the travelers and their surroundings from the descriptions in one of these chapters.

Journey to the Center of the Earth

Chapters 40 to 43

Before you read the chapters:

In the coming chapters Axel and Professor Lidenbrock discuss the amazing timing and "luck" of the events of their journey. Tell about a time when you felt you were very lucky, your timing was perfect or something was "meant" to happen just the way it did for a reason.

_____
_____
_____
_____

Vocabulary:

Write the meanings of each of these words from the novel then find them in the word search.

1. brandish: _____

2. stupefaction: _____

3. insensibility: _____

4. vagaries: _____

5. crags: _____

6. dithyrambics: _____

7. sagacity: _____

8. loiter: _____

9. loath: _____

10. inanition: _____

11. inappreciable: _____

12. masticating: _____

Journey to the Center of the Earth

```
h m x y h e q h i s x g n a k n y l j i d a r n o
y t b b j x l k y l a v i v n k t s x a a u e y e
q t d g w c d b i t p i u s n k i c i o a s f j l
h v p t x u i x a r i w b x b v l j x z g u p b c
u m x g q l s w y i l c f a n y i q p a v e q o z
s e s r g t n r n v c f a d o p b i r r j t e l p
b v f l g f f c l o b e w g e g i c a v n x n j c
v y x m b m w c q h r u r i a j s m p d p b e p q
n g l d h m p s u p a k y p n s n i t q k r g m f
e n u i a m l w h s n d u p p z e c p b a l c g n
x u y i m a v r y m d b f w p a s j p b h c p w r
s n y e m g g e l r i n x w x m n h e u k c k l r
q s e i r a g a v w s x d a r v i n o m n i r j r
k e v y w d s x c j h y g u m h v h i o n h e e l
s l q j c c r t l n e d s g s x u h i a u f t k d
p y a a b o k m i a d y v o z s r t u w p k i h h
w g z q y c l p d c j h g a r w c i h x h j o y q
d c b j w f e a h h a e l z r a t b h f o u l b c
t w a y l o x v h s o t r r f i z u g k u s o k c
c x b e b t y l r y p z i e o l l w z j j i e h e
d i t h r y a m b i c s p n i c c j g c a f c u k
w e y k s a e j z y j u b m g i a g t i y u h e g
s h d o l k f k r r t x a b c c f m c l o m g w y
s o f g z q m d j s i x o p q m w r n v w s o f l
l o a t h h j q y o j o r b z o l p w j r j q c l
```

Questions:

1. In Chapter 40 the travelers come across some new amazing animals and another being. Tell what they see and describe them.

   _____

   _____

   _____

2. Describe the emotional state that Axel and the Professor were in as they walked along their new surroundings in Chapter 40.

   _____

   _____

Journey to the Center of the Earth

3. What did they find in Chapter 40 and what did they realize as a result?

_____

_____

4. What does the Professor mean when he says on page 186, "Yes, Axel, there is really some providential guidance which brought us, going south, back to north, and to Cape Saknussemm."?

_____

_____

5. How has Axel's attitude now changed since the beginning of the journey?

_____

6. What obstacle do they come to when they attempt to follow Saknussemm's path and how do they try to get beyond it?

_____

_____

7. What happens when they attempt to blow up the boulder?

_____

_____

8. Once they pass through the initial passage what happens to them?

_____

9. How fast and at what rate do they estimate they are ascending at? What other form of travel could you compare this speed with?

_____

_____

10. Why did they finally choose to eat what little remained of their food?

_____

11. What are Professor Lidenbrock's exact words when Axel asks if he believes they still have a chance of surviving?

_____

12. What do they believe they are traveling through and what do they notice about the water they are traveling on?

_____

 # Journey to the Center of the Earth

Language Activities:

1. Search the chapters to find ten examples of words of each of the following parts of speech.

Nouns	Verbs	Adjectives	Adverbs	Pronouns
_____	_____	_____	_____	_____
_____	_____	_____	_____	_____
_____	_____	_____	_____	_____
_____	_____	_____	_____	_____
_____	_____	_____	_____	_____
_____	_____	_____	_____	_____
_____	_____	_____	_____	_____
_____	_____	_____	_____	_____
_____	_____	_____	_____	_____
_____	_____	_____	_____	_____

Journey to the Center of the Earth

Extension Activities:

Design a cover that could have been used for this novel. Consider the events, characters, and places from the novel.

Journey to the Center of the Earth

Chapters 44 to 46

Before you read the chapters:

In these chapters our travelers reach the end of their journey and feel a sense of accomplishment because of what they have done for the scientific community. Think of something in your life you have accomplished. Tell what it was and how you felt. If you cannot think of anything write about something you would like to accomplish in your future and how you will feel when you do accomplish it.

_____
_____
_____
_____
_____
_____

Vocabulary:

a) prognostication	____	a mischievous child in ragged dress
b) hyperborean	____	unwilling to believe
c) urchin	____	taking pleasure in
d) contemptuous	____	disturbed
e) revelling	____	moving in a circle
f) credence	____	showing hatred, spite
g) incredulity	____	a prediction
h) detonations	____	a group of islands
i) derangement	____	inhabitant of a northern region
j) proposition	____	an offer
k) gyratory	____	belief in something
l) archipelago	____	explosions

Questions:

1. What did Axel notice about the compass?

_____

Journey to the Center of the Earth

2. Describe the sounds the group hears as they travel.

   _____

3. What did Axel at first believe was happening as they were ascending?

   _____

4. What did Professor Lidenbrock believe was happening and why does he think it is the best thing that could have happened to them?

   _____

   _____

5. What part of the Earth did they think they were ascending to? _____

6. Approximately how long did it take for them to ascend and where and how did they finally arrive back on the surface of the Earth?

   _____

   _____

7. Where did they finally arrive at the end of their ascent and how did they find out where they were?

   _____

   _____

8. What does Axel say on page 207 when he compares the land from which they began their journey to the land which they arrived at upon finally completing their journey?

   _____

   _____

9. How were the travelers treated by the people and fishermen of Stromboli?

   _____

10. How did they relay the events of their journey to the scientific community?

    _____

11. How did the world receive the claims of Professor Lidenbrock and the stories of their journey?

    _____

    _____

12. The recordings of the compass during their journey were puzzling them even after the journey ended. What turned out to be the problem with the compass and how did they notice?

_____

_____

13. How does Axel describe their life after this journey at the very end of the novel?

_____

_____

_____

Language Activities:

Literary Elements:

Climax: The turning point in a story, where something may suddenly go terribly wrong or a dramatic change takes place.

Conflict: A struggle between opposing forces. Conflicts can exist between characters or inside a character's mind.

Setting: The time and place where a story occurs. It can be specific or general. It affects the story events.

After reading about these literary elements answer the following questions:

1. What is the climax of this story?

_____

2. What are the major conflicts that occur in this story?

_____

_____

_____

3. When and where is this story set and how does the setting affect the events of the story?

_____

_____

_____

_____

Journey to the Center of the Earth

4. Use the diagram below to compare and contrast the similarities and differences between *Journey to the Center of the Earth* in novel form and in movie form.

How is the movie different?

_____
_____
_____
_____
_____
_____
_____
_____
_____
_____

How are the movie and novel alike?

_____
_____
_____
_____
_____
_____
_____
_____
_____
_____

How is the novel different?

_____
_____
_____
_____
_____
_____
_____
_____
_____
_____

Journey to the Center of the Earth

Extension Activities:

1. Timeline:

In pairs or small groups create a timeline of the events of the travelers. You will need a long poster. Draw some pictures pertaining to the events of the timeline.

2. Skits:

Write and perform a skit for your class. Choose from the three ideas below or come up with an idea of your own that you have agreed upon with your teacher. You might want to video record your skit if possible or perform it live.

- Conduct an interview with a character or characters of your choice.

- Present a newscast that might have been aired after Professor Lidenbrock, Axel and Hans returned with news of their journey.

- Create a commercial enticing people to travel to one of the places the travelers visited on their journey.

Answer Key

Chapters 1 to 4: *(page 12)*

Before you Read:
1. Some words and phrases will sound/read unusual to native English speakers. Some of the meaning may be changed slightly.
2. Answers may vary but may include the Earth's mineral makeup, the layers of the Earth, the temperature is very hot, etc.

Vocabulary:
Answers may vary.

Questions:
1. Hamburg, Germany
2. intelligent, serious, hard working, impatient, a miser, a savant, passionate, stubborn, curious, persistent, not a good speaker, etc. He was a curator at the museum. The townspeople laughed at him and the difficulty he had speaking to an audience.
3. made of brick and stone, leaned forward, etc. Axel, Martha (the cook) and Grauben (Lidenbrock's godchild) lived with him.
4. Axel is an orphan, he wants to please his uncle, he admires his uncle, he is passionate about science, he is perceptive and intelligent, he likes to eat, he is in love with Grauben.
5. It was bound in cowhide, yellowish, with a faded tassel, still in good shape.
6. Axel and the Professor as described in questions 2 and 4. They are a lot alike!
7. Grauben and Axel were betrothed to be married.
8. Axel is fanning himself with the parchment. He is terrified, does not want his uncle to know and plans to destroy the parchment.

Language Activity:
Answers may vary.
tone – exciting, fun
mood – excited, anxious
point of view – first person
foreshadowing: page 9 – "This bodes something serious' went on the old servant, shaking her head."
page 16 – "I had the presentiment of some approaching catastrophe."

Extension:
Answers may vary.

Chapters 5 to 8: *(page 16)*

Vocabulary:
3, 11, 5, 21, 25, 7, 24, 20, 23, 16, 4, 18, 10, 1, 6, 13, 14, 15, 12, 19, 9, 22, 17, 8, 2

Questions:
1. Axel did not want his uncle to know the message as he knew he would want to go to the center of the Earth and probably take Axel with him.
2. about 24 hours; he found that the professor had locked them in
3. a) Axel didn't really believe they could get to the center of the Earth and thought they may be in danger if they went.
   b) Answers may vary.
4. He had never heard of Snaefell or Scaratis, he didn't believe one could enter the volcano, Jokul, he didn't know what the calends of July had to do with it all, and he doubted that Arne Saknussemm had actually made it to the center of the Earth.
5. Answers may vary.
6. "Go dear Axel. You are leaving your betrothed, but you will find your wife when you come back."
7. they got on the train at Altona at 7:00 am, arrived at Kiel at 10:00am, left Kiel at 10:00 pm, arrived at Korsor at 7:00 a.m. the next day, arrived at Copenhagen, Denmark at 10 am
8. He wished Grauben was with him.
9. a) He wanted them to get accustomed to heights.
   b) Axel was afraid of heights and was dizzy the entire time and exhausted at the end.
   c) 5 days in a row
10. The Valkyria, M. Bjorne, Sunday at 7 am.

Language Activities:
1. Leyden jar is a device to store electric charge.   2. Answers may vary.

Extension:
1. 2 432 902 009 175 640 000   2. Answers may vary.

Chapters 9 to 12: *(page 20)*

Vocabulary: Answers may vary.

1. luxurious
2. clay, pottery
3. ash from burnt minerals
4. high rank
5. evil
6. sluggish
7. exact timepiece for use at sea
8. supplies
9. go beyond limits
10. predict

Questions:

1. It would help the professor get anything he needs on his journey.
2. **a)** He was seasick.
   b) that he deserved to be sick for going on this journey and being so difficult
3. Answers will vary.
4. **a)** They pass them on to the next person without returning them to the library and read them well.
   b) He says they prefer to wear books out by reading than sitting on shelves.
5. He was persecuted for heresy and his books were burnt.
6. He didn't want anyone to know what he was doing.
7. Answers may vary.
8. a thermometer, manometer, chronometer, 2 compasses, a night glass, 2 Ruhmkorff's apparatus, 4 guns, 2 pickaxes, 2 spades, a rope ladder, 3 iron sticks, a hatchet, hammer, 12 wedges and iron holdfasts, ropes, food – essence of beef, dry biscuits, gin, gourds for water, a medicine chest, some tobacco, hunting powder, tinder, a pack, money, paper, good boots
9. He means he is beginning to enjoy this journey.
10. No, he doesn't. At the start of Chapter 12 he states his belief that Saknussem did not go there; it is just a hoax.

Language Activities:

1. Reik-i-a-vik, sump-tu-ous, Val-kyr-i-a, suff-ra-gan, min-er-a-log-i-cal, di-a-bol-i-cal, pre-cip-i-tous, man-o-me-ter, pro-vi-sions
2. Answers may vary.
3. **a)** Hamlet is a character in a Shakespearean play; he was insane.
   b) Horace was a Roman poet who spoke Latin.
   c) Virgil was also a Roman poet, who is considered good fortune to travelers.

Chapters 13 to 16: *(page 27)*

Vocabulary:

1. food, animal feed
2. silence
3. ghost
4. gesture, motion
5. underground
6. leafy
7. period
8. indirect, winding
9. small
10. lump (or other acceptable synonyms)

Questions:

1. the way they prepared food, they were poor, house full of children, different customs and language, etc.
2. They were lepers who had swollen heads, were bald and were covered in sores.
3. He was afraid Snaefell would awaken and erupt; Professor said he had thought of it and was making observations and asking questions already that led him to believe it would not erupt.
4. The rector was rude and charged them too much.
5. Axel had difficulty; Professor supported him.
6. Hans saw it coming and directed them to safety.
7. a mortar (the barrel of a gun or cannon)
8. He needed sun to see the shadow that would guide him.
9. Sunday, June 28, the sun finally came out

Language Activities:

hypotheses, axes, bacilli, fungi, radii, phenomena, bacteria, vortices

Chapters 17 to 20: *(page 30)*
Vocabulary:

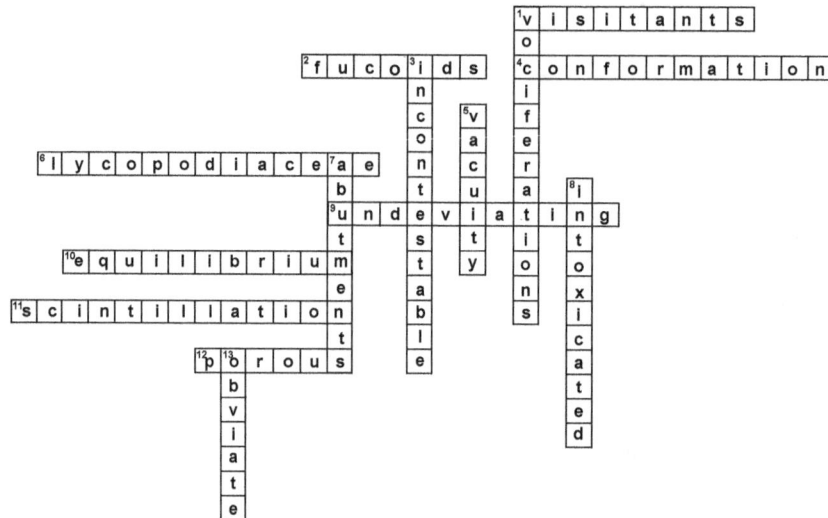

Questions:
1. being "drawn" to falling
2. the idea that the earth gets hotter as you go deeper inside it; by traveling to the Earth's center
3. exceeded by 6 000 feet the greatest depth ever achieved by man
4. He knew it was entirely up to chance and there was no use wasting time; he is decisive and intellectual.
5. They are entering into a different period and going in the wrong direction.
6. from Tuesday to Saturday (5 days)
7. They would be out of water the next day.

Language Activities:
1. coolly
2. frantically
3. quicker
4. slowly
5. rapidly
6. heartily
7. bravely
8. carefully

Chapters 21 to 24: *(page 33)*
Vocabulary:
Sentences may vary.

Questions:
1. He saved it for Axel.
2. to continue on this path for one more day and if they do not find water they will return to the surface of Earth
3. He thinks he is leaving them; then, he realizes he would be going the wrong way to go back up.
4. They hear the water running; Hans uses his pickaxe to create a hole in the wall.
5. **a)** 30 leagues from Iceland   **b)** 2 ½ leagues   **c)** under the Atlantic Ocean
6. When it was foaming and angry it reminded Axel of his uncle's passion; in its calm, continuous flow it reminded him of Hans.

Language Activities:
1. swollen
2. trembling
3. big
4. harsh, threatening
5. deep
6. quiet
7. precious
8. brave
9. zealous
10. determined
11. easier
12. solid

Chapters 25 to 28: *(page 36)*
Vocabulary:
f, l, e, d, c, i, k, h, g, a, b, j

Questions:
1. the end of the Earth's crust
2. The air would turn solid.
3. You stop thinking in words and ideas.
4. He became dramatic and hopeless.
5. find and follow the stream (Hansbach)
6. Answers may vary.
7. an acoustic effect – the wall conducted the sound of their voices

Language Activities:
d (p 16), a (p 34), b (p 49), g (p 44), c (p 78), e (p 118), f (p 105)

Chapters 29 to 32: *(page 39)*

Vocabulary:

1. adorned
2. cicatrized
3. inanimate
4. undulation
5. counterscarp
6. irradiated
7. aurora borealis
8. ascertained
9. cognisance
10. invigoration
11. declivities
12. rivulets
13. promontory
14. antediluvian
15. menagerie
16. arborescent
17. delirium
18. scrutinized

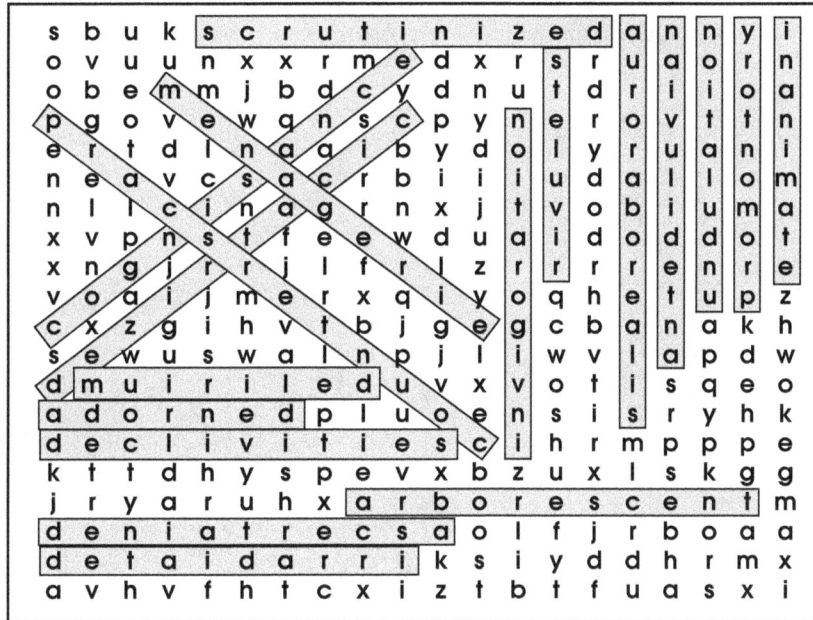

```
s b u k s c r u t i n i z e d a n n y i
o v u u n x x r m e d x r s r u a o r n
o b e m m j b d c y d n u t d r i i o a
p g o v e w a n s c p y n e r o v t t n
e r t d i n a i b y d o l y r u a n i m
n e a v c s a c r b i i u d a l l o a
n l i c i n a g r n x j t v o b i u m a
x v p n s t f e e w d u a i d o d d o t
x n g j r j l f r l z r r r e n r e
v o a i m e r x q i y o q h e t u p z
c x z g i h v t b j g e g c b a n a k h
s e w u s w a n p j l i w v l a p d w
d m u i r i l e d u v x v o t i s q e o
a d o r n e d p l u o e n s i s r y h k
d e c l i v i t i e s c i h r m p p p e
k t t d h y s p e v x b z u x l s k g g
j r y a r u h x a r b o r e s c e n t m
d e n i a t r e c s a o l f j r b o a a
d e t a i d a r r i k s i y d d h r m x
a v h v f h t c x i z t b t f u a s x i
```

Questions:

1. Axel means that the Professor doesn't usually show emotions such as affection, until a crisis.
2. He seemed to be near a sea and there was a natural light above.
3. prehistoric animals such as mastodons
4. the needle would stand up
5. fossil wood they found on the beach
6. Professor proposes naming it Port Axel; Axel suggests Port Grauben.
7. a fish similar to a sturgeon

Chapters 33 to 36: *(page 42)*

Vocabulary:

e, b, j, o, p, d, n, h, a, c, i, f, k, l, g, m

Questions:

1. He feels they are wasting time on the water and he is not sure if this is the right route.
2. to see how deep the sea is, there were teeth marks on the pickaxe when they brought it back up – telling them there were other animals below
3. "extinct" fish
4. The ichthyosaurus had the face of a porpoise, head of a lizard, teeth of a crocodile and the shape of a whale; the plesiosaurus was snake-like with a turtle's shell and claws like oars. The reptiles attacked each other.
5. Axel thought they were sailing towards a massive animal spouting water; it turned out to be an island with a geyser.
6. under England
7. air is oppressive, the sea is calm, atmosphere is saturated with electrical fluid
8. it is a fiery disc, it magnetizes all their tools and the raft
9. Answers may vary.

Chapters 37 to 39: *(page 45)*

Vocabulary: Student definitions may vary.

1. increase
2. cannot be heard
3. spread throughout
4. flood
5. oddities
6. change from
7. threatening
8. relinquish one's own rights and will
9. an item from the past
10. receptacle for bones
11. oppose
12. protruding jaw

Questions:

1. only their firearms; minor bumps, bruises, and injuries
2. find a new route or return the way they came

3. that during the storm they had gotten turned around and returned to the same shore from which they left
4. that their raft was not able to withstand the sea and the storm again
5. The water finds its way into the Earth through fissures under the ocean and the water is partly vaporized by subterranean fires, which causes the electrical activity.
6. a human skull
7. A human jawbone was found in France, 14 feet below surface and proved that man existed longer ago then at first thought, at the time of prehistoric animals; the skull they found further proves this claim.
8. They could have recorded or photographed their findings and possibly even communicated it live to someone on the Earth's surface.

Chapters 40 to 43: *(page 50)*
Vocabulary:
Definitions may vary.

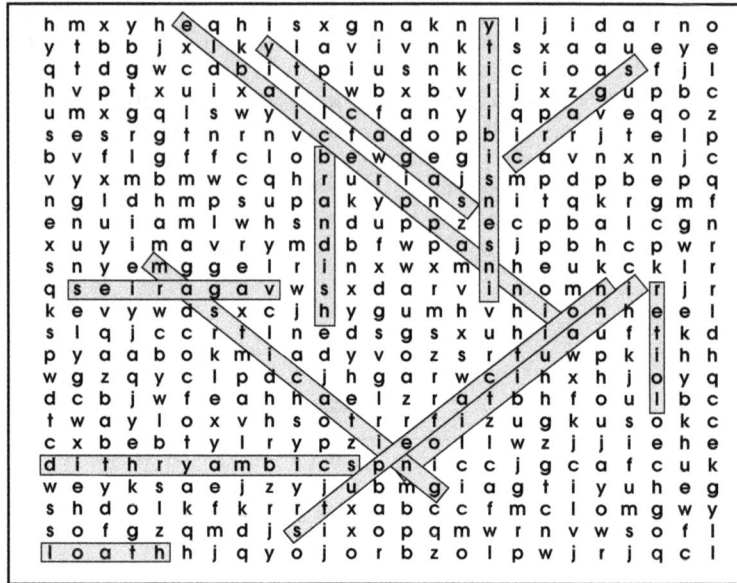

```
h m x y h e q h i s x g n a k n y l j i d a r n o
y t b b j x l k y l a v i v n k t s x a a u e y e
q t d g w c d b t p i u s n k i c i o a s f j l
h v p t x u i x a r w b x b v l j x z g u p b c
u m x g q l s w y i c f a n y i q p a v e q o z
s e s r g t n r n v c t a d o p b i r j t e l p
b v f l g f f c l o b e w g e g i c a v n x n j c
v y x m b m w c q h r u r i a j s m p d p b e p q
n g l d h m p s u p a k y p n s n i t q k r g m f
e n u i a m l w h s n d u p p z e c p b a l c g n
x u y i m a v r y m d b f w p a s j p b h c p w r
s n y e m g g e l r i n x w x m n h e u k c k l r
q s e i r a g a v w s x d a r v i n o m n l r j r
k e v y w d s x c j h y g u m h v h o n h e e l
s l q j c c r l n e d s g s x u h a u f t k d
p y a a b o k m i a d y v o z s r t u w p k i h h
w g z q y c l p d c j h g a r w c i x h j o y q
d c b j w f e a h h a e l z r a t b h f o u l b c
t w a y l o x v h s o r r l i z u g k u s o k c
c x b e b t y l r y p z i e o l w z j j i e h e
d i t h r y a m b i c s p n i c c j g c a f c u k
w e y k s a e j z y u b m g i a g t i y u h e g
s h d o l k f k r r x a b c c f m c l o m g w y
s o f g z q m d j s i x o p q m w r n v w s o f l
l o a t h h j q y o j o r b z o l p w j r j q c l
```

Questions:
1. mastodons and a large man   2. astonished, stupefied
3. a knife belonging to Arne Saknussem and his initials written on a block of granite
4. Some power bigger than themselves is leading them.
5. He has the same excitement and passion now as his uncle and the desire to go further and find all they can.
6. a boulder in their way; they blow it up   7. The water and their raft were thrown into a hole.
8. They begin to rise.
9. a rate of 12 feet per second, 90 miles an hour; compared to a speeding car or a train
10. they needed their strength
11. "while the heart beats and the flesh palpitates, a creature endowed with will should never give place to despair"
12. a fissure in the rock; the water is extremely hot

Chapters 44 to 46: *(page 55)*
Vocabulary: c,g,e,i,k,d,a,l,b,j,f,h

Questions:
1. It was spinning.   2. like detonations
3. an earthquake
4. They were being forced out of a volcano; it would be the quickest way for them to reach the Earth's surface.
5. a northern area of Earth   6. it took them all night
7. Stromboli, Italy; from a little boy
8. "we left the region of eternal snows for those of infinite verdure: and exchanged the grey fogs of frozen zone for the azure blue of a Sicilian sky"   9. They were helpful, generous and hospitable.
10. an announcement at the museum where the Professor worked
11. There were mixed feelings – some believed and some did not.
12. the pole of the compass was magnetized by the fireball while on the sea; they noticed awhile after returning
13. Axel marries Grauben and the Professor becomes a member of every possible scientific community and is famous; they are all happy.

Language Activities:
1. the rise to the surface of the Earth
2. inner conflict within Axel; conflict between his uncle and himself over whether to go on this journey; man vs. nature
3. inside the Earth – allows the author to create new, never seen worlds from his imagination

www.ingramcontent.com/pod-product-compliance
Lightning Source LLC
Chambersburg PA
CBHW080523090426
42734CB00015B/3144